UNDER THE MICROSCOPE

OCEAN LIFE

Casey Horton

Gareth Stevens Publishing
MILWAUKEE

For a free color catalog describing Gareth Stevens Publishing's list of high-quality books and multimedia programs, call 1-800-542-2595 (USA) or 1-800-461-9120 (Canada). Gareth Stevens Publishing's Fax: (414) 225-0377. See our catalog, too, on the World Wide Web: http://gsinc.com

Library of Congress Cataloging-in-Publication Data

Horton, Casey.
    Ocean life / by Casey Horton.
      p. cm. – (Under the microscope)
    Includes index.
    Summary: Presents the tiny creatures floating in the ocean, the sparkling eyes of a scallop, and other microscopic marvels of the sea.
    ISBN 0-8368-1606-4 (lib. bdg.)
    1. Marine animals–Juvenile literature. 2. Marine plants–Juvenile literature.
  3. Microscopy–Juvenile literature. [1. Marine animals. 2. Marine plants.
  3. Microscopy.] I. Title. II. Series.
  QL122.2.H67 1997
  591.92–dc20   96-34481

First published in North America in 1997 by
Gareth Stevens Publishing
1555 North RiverCenter Drive, Suite 201
Milwaukee, WI 53212 USA

© 1997 Brown Packaging Partworks Ltd., 255-257 Liverpool Road, London, England, N1 1LX. Text by Casey Horton. Photos supplied by — page 27: Biophoto Associates; pages 5, 13, 19, 21, 23: Frank Lane Picture Agency; page 17: Oxford Scientific Films; pages 7, 9, 15, 25, 29: Science Photo Library; page 11: Tony Stone Images. Additional end matter © 1997 by Gareth Stevens, Inc.

Printed in the United States of America

1 2 3 4 5 6 7 8 9 01 00 99 98 97

CONTENTS

LINK IN THE CHAIN

The vast oceans of the planet Earth contain many thousands of types of tiny plants and animals called plankton. Many of these plants and animals are so small they can be seen only with a microscope or magnifying glass. Scientists have given plant plankton the name *phytoplankton*. These plants are very important to all other forms of ocean life. Many sea creatures, both large and small, feed on phytoplankton. These plant-eating creatures are, in turn, eaten by animals that feed on other animals.

Phytoplankton constantly floats and drifts on the surface of the ocean. These tiny plants are driven by the force of wind and waves. Sea creatures eat them.

ON THE SEAFLOOR

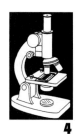

- A large part of phytoplankton is made up of plants called diatoms. Diatoms contain silica, a hard mineral. When diatoms die and decay, the silica collects on the seafloor. There it forms a white, powdery material called diatomite.

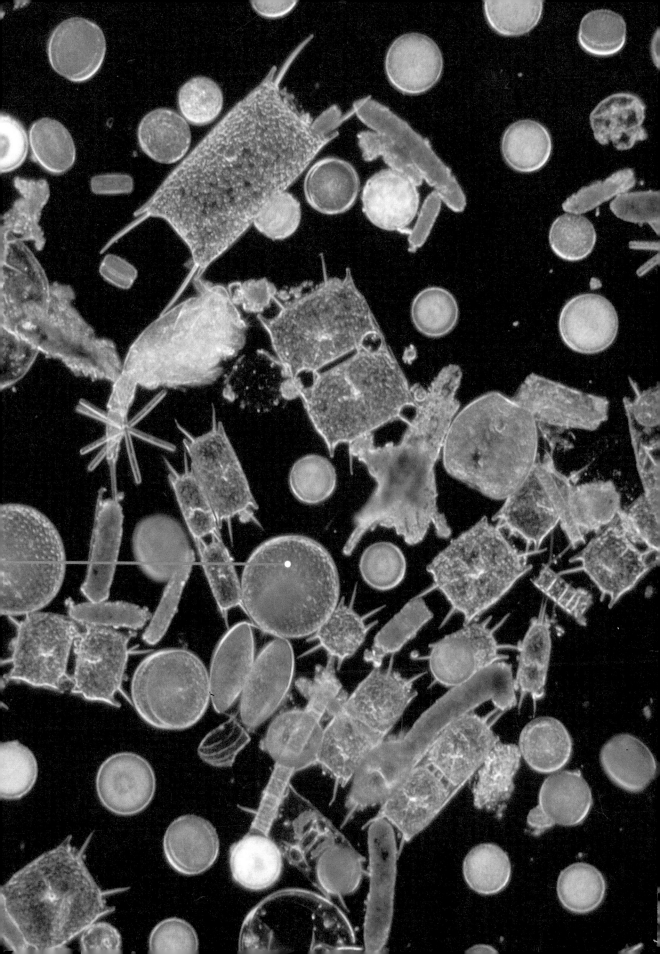

SPIRALING SEASHELLS

Scientists have given animal plankton the name *zooplankton*. Some types of zooplankton are protected by a chalky shell. One of these creatures is known as globigerina. Globigerina makes a shell that forms a round cavity, or room. As the animal grows larger, it makes more and more cavities, each one bigger than the last one. The cavities form clusters that are arranged in a spiral. The entire spiral is surrounded by long spines. Both the cavities as well as the spines contain a liquid that keeps the globigerina afloat.

Pictured is a cluster of round shells made by a growing globigerina. The animal is extremely tiny at first. The cluster may grow to only the size of a pinhead.

A MUDDY OOZE

- The empty shells of globigerina drop to the seafloor when the animals inside them die. There they form a chalky mud called marine ooze. The ooze covers about one-third of the entire seafloor. In some places, it may be hundreds of feet (meters) thick.

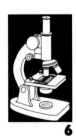

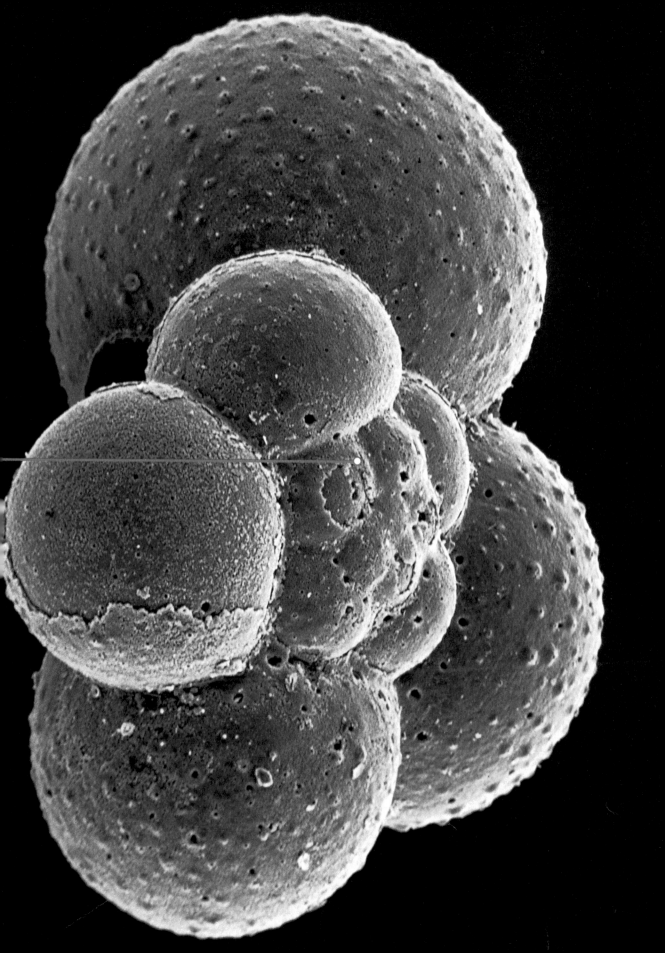

GLASSY SCULPTURE

Diatoms are tiny green or brown phytoplankton. Over a thousand different kinds exist. Like most of Earth's other plants, diatoms contain a substance called chlorophyll. Chlorophyll helps diatoms gather energy from sunlight, which is used to make food. Diatoms have only one cell, divided into two parts. One part fits the other like a lid on a box. A hard material called silica in the cell wall becomes sculpted into fascinating shapes at times.

The two parts of a diatom can be seen clearly in this photograph. The diatom's glassy appearance comes from the material called silica that makes up its cell wall.

RICHES FROM THE OCEAN

• Over millions and millions of years, layer after layer of dead plankton and other materials have deposited themselves on the seafloor. The sediment that forms becomes compressed and heated from the weight of the layers, eventually changing into oil and gas.

SHARK STORY

Sharks belong to a group of animals called cartilaginous fish. These fish have skeletons made of gristle, or cartilage. With other types of fish, such as cod, goldfish, or trout, the skeleton is made of bone. Bony fish lay masses of eggs that are released into the water. They float back and forth until they develop into small fish. But with most sharks, the eggs develop while they are still inside the mother's body. When sharks are born, they look like completely developed, but smaller, versions of the adults.

This young shark is growing inside of its mother's body. The round object is called the placenta. It is a food source for the growing shark until it is born.

KING OF THE SHARKS

- The whale shark is the largest shark and the largest of all the fish. It grows to about 50 feet (15 m) long. The whale shark feeds mainly on phytoplankton and small fish.

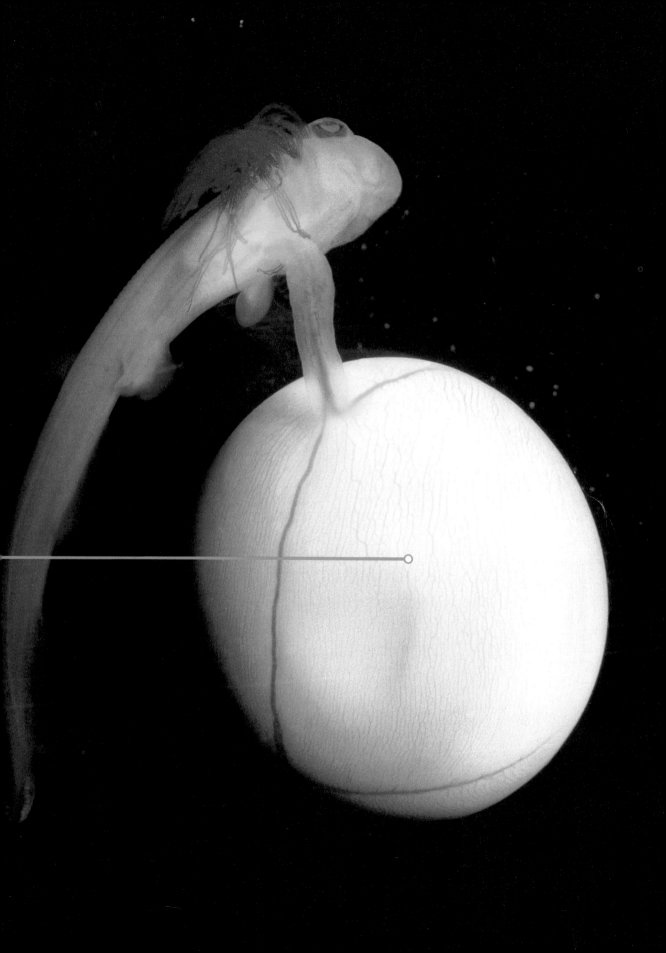

SPEEDY SWIMMERS

Mollusks are sea creatures found throughout the oceans of Earth. Squid belong to the group of mollusks called cephalopods. This is a Greek word meaning "head-footed." In the squid, the "foot" is divided into 8–10 arms that circle the head. Over short distances, the squid is one of the fastest swimmers of all the ocean creatures. It has a long, streamlined body. It moves by sending out a powerful jet of water from a special tube in its body. Squid have well-developed brains and are thought to be intelligent.

These dwarf squid are newly hatched. Young squid look exactly like the adults, only smaller. Immediately after hatching, squid swim to the surface of the water.

GREAT LENGTHS

• Most squid are small, reaching a length of about 1 foot (30 centimeters). The largest is the giant squid that lives in the North Atlantic. It can grow up to 55 feet (17 m) in length.

WHELK WARRIORS

A whelk is a snail with a shell that coils around and around, ending in a point. The shells often wash up on the ocean's shore. Empty egg cases of the dog whelk can also be found along the tide line. Dog whelks attach their long, torpedo-shaped egg cases to rocks. Each case may have 24 to 36 eggs inside it. When the young whelks hatch, they crawl out of the open end of the case. Dog whelks live under rocks on beaches. They feed on other animals, especially barnacles. They drill through the barnacle's shell with a long organ called a proboscis.

The dog whelk's proboscis contains a long tongue called a radula. The radula contains rows of tiny, sharp teeth that rasp, or file, food from inside shells.

NO DENTISTS NECESSARY

• Unlike human beings, who have only two sets of teeth in a lifetime, the whelk produces a brand new set of teeth whenever the old ones wear out.

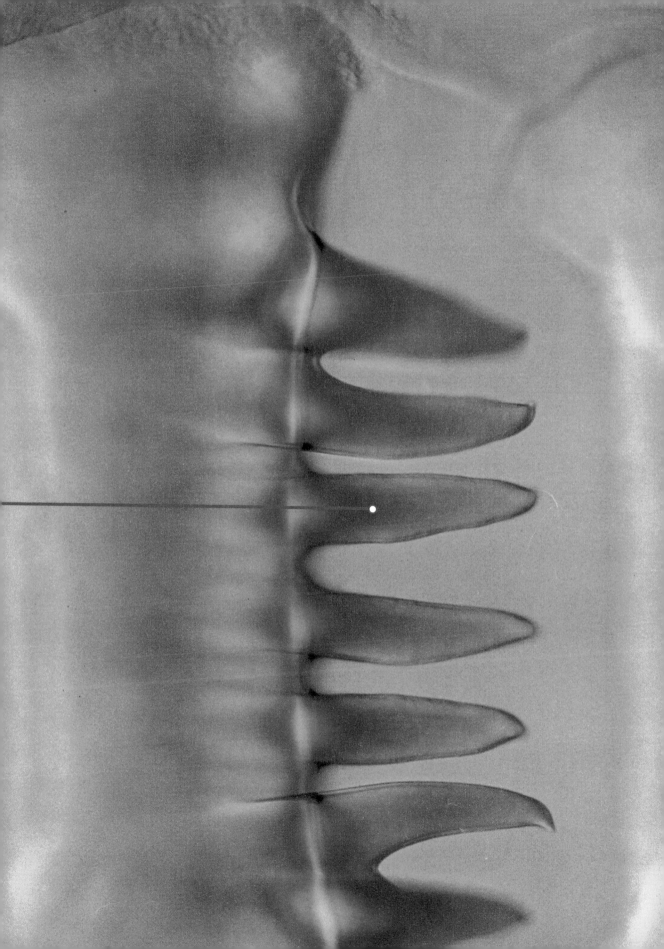

FAN-SHAPED BEAUTIES

Sea creatures called scallops have two fan-shaped shells joined on one side by a hinge. Scallops are also known as *fan shells*. One shell is rounded, and the other is flat. The shells of a scallop come in beautiful colors and various patterns. The scallop swims by clapping its two shells together. This forces a jet of water out of the shell, which pushes the scallop forward or backward. In this way, it can try to escape from its worst enemy — the starfish.

Pictured are the edges of a scallop shell. The two edges are fringed with a ring of tentacles and studded with little eyes. Each of the eyes has a sparkling lens.

HEADLESS WONDERS

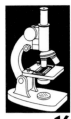

- Scallops have eyes and a mouth, but no head. The mouth opens directly into the body, and the scallop gathers its food through a tube at the back of its body.

PARALYZING BEAUTY

Sea anemones are often mistaken for plants. But they are actually animals. They seem like plants because they are attached to rocks or the seafloor and do not move around. A sea anemone is made of two parts — a ring of tentacles that circles the mouth and a column that is like a blob of jelly. When their tentacles are extended, sea anemones look like pretty flowers. Although they may seem inviting, sea anemones are deadly to the shrimp on which they feed.

These dainty "fingers" are a sea anemone's tentacles. Some anemones withdraw their tentacles when they are touched. Others have tentacles that cannot be withdrawn.

BEAUTIFUL, BUT DEADLY

• Among a sea anemone's tentacles are small *U*-shaped organs that each contains a coiled stinger. When a shrimp swims into the center of the anemone, the anemone paralyzes the shrimp using the stinger. The anemone then drags the shrimp into the opening that leads to its stomach.

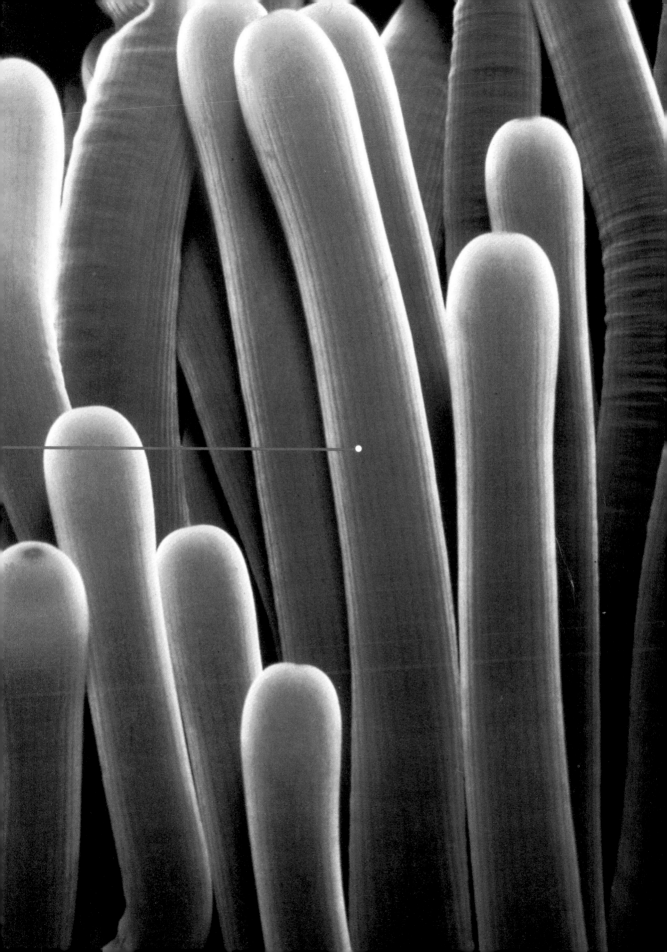

HEDGEHOGS OF THE SEA

Sea urchins belong to a group of sea animals called echinoderms. This name comes from a Greek word meaning "hedgehog spines," referring to the spines on each animal's hard outer covering. Although it is called a shell, this hard covering is actually the skeleton that protects the animal's soft body parts. The sea urchin usually lives at the bottom of the ocean on top of gravel beds, but it sometimes comes in close to the beach. It remains in place during stormy seas, clinging tightly to rocks.

Pictured is the underside of a sea urchin. The animal's mouth and teeth can be seen in the center of the shell, or skeleton. The skeleton protects the sea urchin.

A TASTY MORSEL

- Certain parts of the sea urchin are edible to humans. Some people find the male reproductive organs of the sea urchin to be delicious. These organs are often referred to as "caviar," like the eggs of the sturgeon fish.

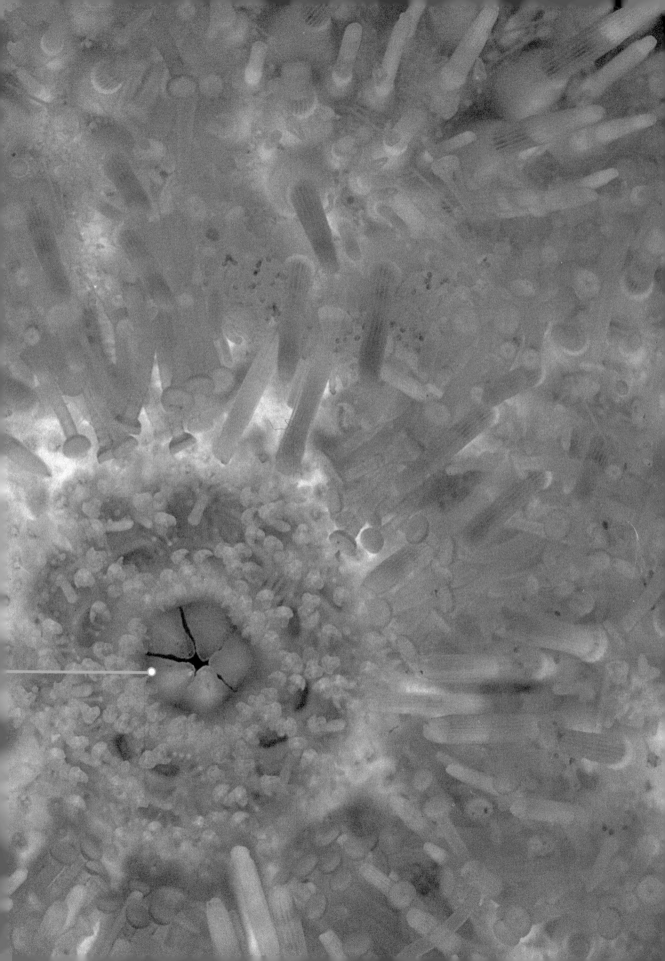

THIS IS A TEST

The hard shell of a sea urchin is known as the "test." One kind is round, but it is flat on the bottom. This is where the urchin's mouth is located. The animal has strong jaws containing sharp teeth that it uses to grind up meals of tiny animals. Sharp spines cover much of the test and are painful to humans if stepped on. The spines usually fall off when the sea urchin dies, so any tests found on the beach are usually spineless.

The sockets pictured on this sea urchin form part of the joints from which spines emerge. Balls on the ends of the spines fit into the sockets, allowing the spines to move.

WALKING ON STILTS

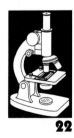

- The sea urchin moves around on tube-shaped feet. Each foot has a sucker on the end that the animal uses to cling to rocks. But the sea urchin can also move on top of flat surfaces by using its spines as if they were stilts.

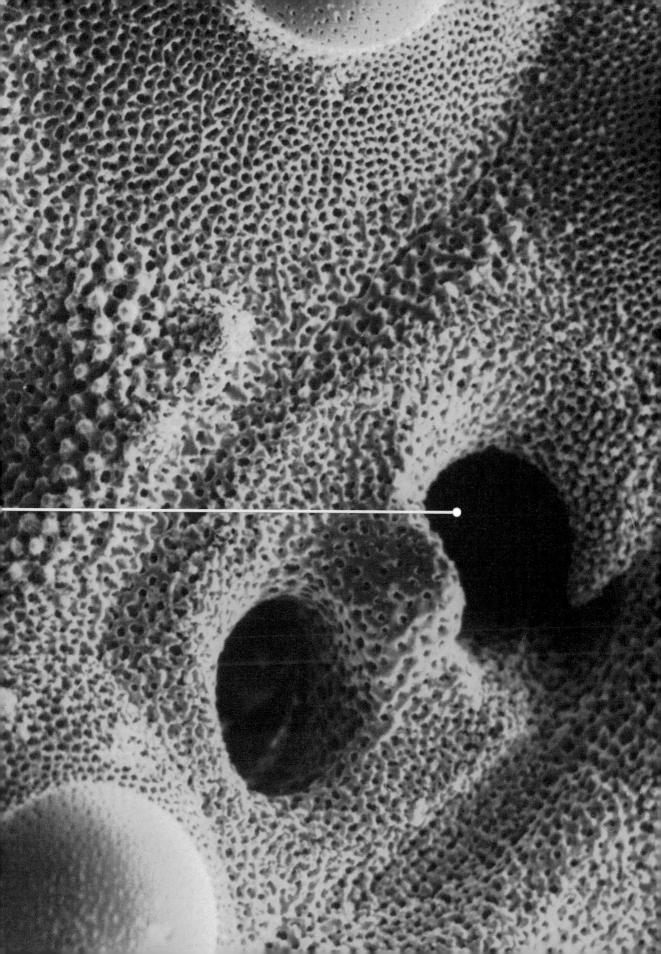

SEA WORMS

Together with shrimp and crabs, other tiny ocean creatures called mystacocardia belong to the group of animals known as crustaceans. Mystacocardia are not very common. In the United States, they can be found mainly on the beaches of Massachusetts and Connecticut. Each has a long body, divided into segments like the body of an earthworm. On the head are antennae, the mouth, and two pairs of mouthparts, which are used to bite and crush food. These animals are blind and get information about their surroundings from small feelers called antennules at the end of their bodies.

The entire body of a mystacocardia can be seen in this photograph. It is covered in cuticle — a thin, shell-like material — similar to the covering found on shrimp.

A SANDY HOME

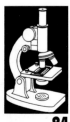

- Mystacocardia live in the seafloor beneath shallow waters. They bury themselves in the sand and swim in water-filled spaces. They feed by filtering tiny particles from the water.

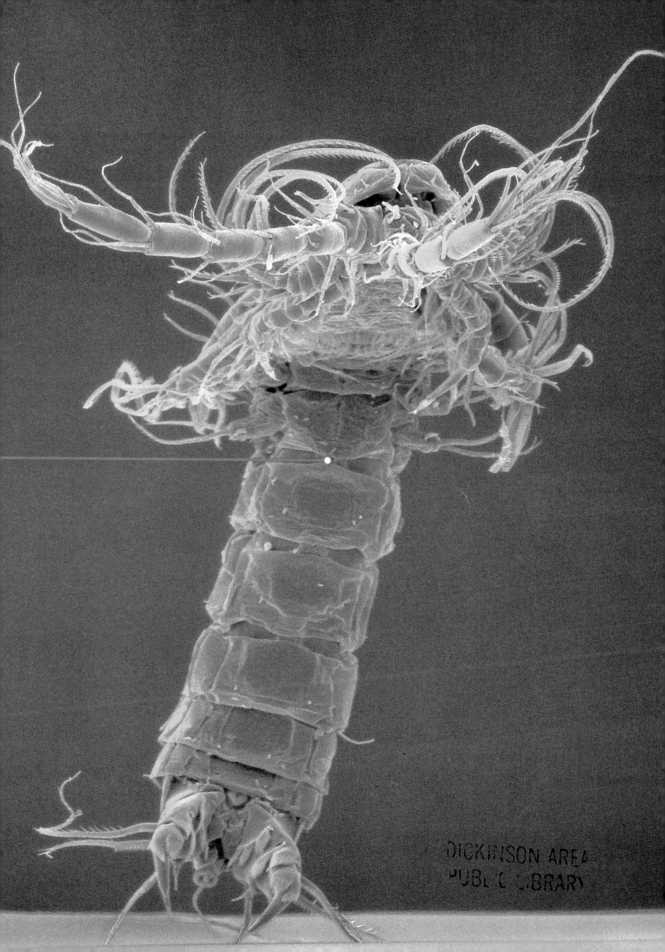

GONE FISHING

The outer layer of a fish's skin, the epidermis, protects its body. The epidermis contains nerves, blood vessels, and sense organs that relay information about the outside world to the fish's brain. Underneath the epidermis is another layer of skin called the dermis. It contains structures that produce the fish's scales. These egg-shaped scales grow larger as the fish grows in size. Each year, another ring is added to the scales. Scientists can tell the age of a fish by counting the number of rings on a scale.

Pictured are fish scales from a sole. The scales are round with projections at the edges. A fish's age can be determined by counting the rings on a scale.

DOUBLE VISION

• The sole and other fish in the group known as flatfish begin life like other fish, with eyes on both sides of their heads. As the sole grows, its body becomes flatter. At the same time, one eye begins to move closer to the other. Eventually, both eyes are on the same side of the head!

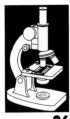

BRISTLING WITH PRIDE

Bristleworms that live in the oceans and on rocky or sandy beaches are close relatives of the earthworm. They get their name from the stiff bristles that grow in pairs along their bodies. Marine bristleworms live under rocks and stones, in muddy sand, among the plankton, and on the seafloor. Some even bore holes in rocks. Others build permanent homes by burrowing in the sand. The bristleworms known as terebellids have a mass of tangled tentacles on their heads. The tentacles are used for breathing and gathering food.

The bristleworm is a microscopic marine worm. Its body is divided into segments. This worm gets its name from the stiff bristles that grow in pairs along its body.

A LIVING FOREST

- Some bristleworms, such as peacock worms, build sand burrows up from the seafloor. The collection of burrows looks like a mini-forest of palm trees. The body of the worm is inside the burrow, but its long tentacles fan out of the top.

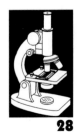

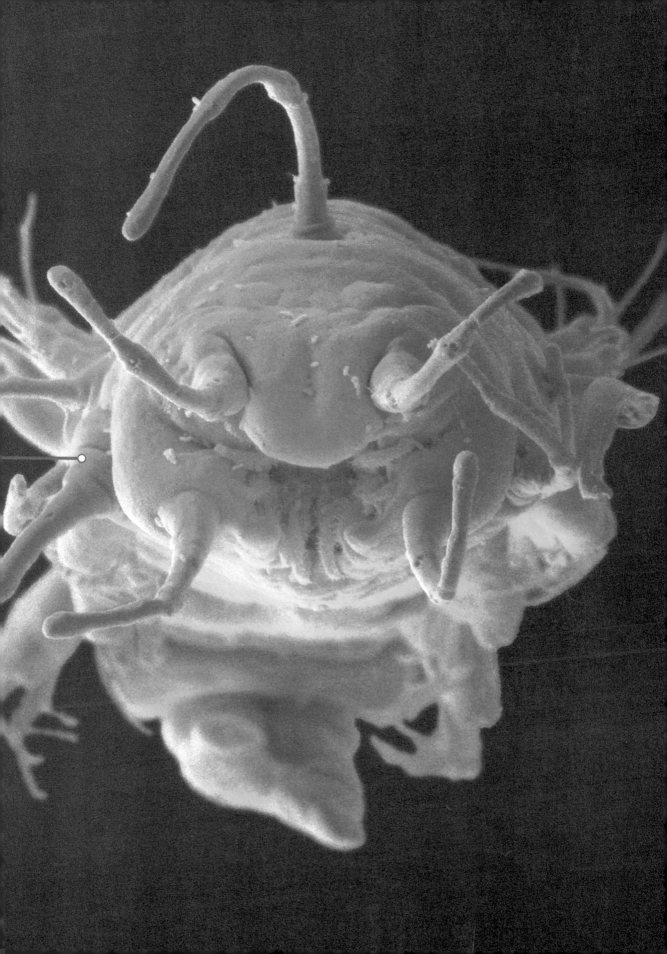

GLOSSARY

antennae: feelers that grow on the heads of some animals.

cavity: a hole. It may be small, like a hole in a tooth; or large, like a hole that is an entrance to a cave.

marine: relating to or living in the world's oceans or seas.

phytoplankton: microscopic plants that live in the world's oceans and seas.

plankton: small plants and animals that float in the sea. The plants in plankton are called phytoplankton. The animals are called zooplankton.

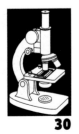

proboscis: a long tube on the head of some animals that is used in the process of feeding.

projections: in animals, objects that stick out from the body.

segment: one of the parts into which an entire object is divided.

silica: a mineral found in some plants and animals, and in the rock known as quartz. Silica is used to make glass and cement.

tentacles: long, arm-like growths on some sea animals, usually found on the head. Tentacles are used by the animals for holding objects and for feeding.

test: the hard outer covering, or shell, found on some animals.

zooplankton: microscopic animals that live in the world's oceans and seas.

FURTHER STUDY

BOOKS

At Home in the Tide Pool. Alexandra Wright
  (Charlesbridge)

Colors of the Sea (series). Ethan/Bearanger
  (Gareth Stevens)

Eco-Journey (series). Behm/Bonar (Gareth Stevens)

Endangered Sea Life! Bob Burton (Gareth Stevens)

Let's Investigate Slippery, Splendid Sea Creatures.
  Madelyn W. Carlisle (Barron)

Mollusks. Joy Richardson (Franklin Watts)

Tentacles: Octopus, Squid and Their Relatives.
  James Martin (Crown)

VIDEOS

Animals and Such (series): Fish. Ocean Animals.
  (Agency for Instructional Technology)

Fish. All About Animals (series). (AIMS Media)

The Microscope. (Encyclopædia Britannica)

Ocean Realm. (United Learning)

*Under the Sea. Children's Video Encyclopedia
  (series).* (Concord Video)

*What's a Fish? What's Under the Ocean? The First
  Time (series).* (Film Ideas, Inc.)

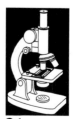

31

INDEX

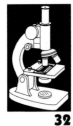